W9-ANX-940

Table of Contents

Golden Retriever Puppies   3

Photo Glossary   15

Index   16

About the Author   16

Rourke
Educational Media

A Division of
Carson Dellosa Education

rourkeeducationalmedia.com

Can you find these words?

ears

golden

puppies

sit

Golden Retriever Puppies

puppies

These are Golden Retriever **puppies!**

What do Golden Retriever puppies look like?

They have long **ears.**

5

They have **golden** fur.

golden

They get big. They grow to 23 inches (58 centimeters) tall.

What do Golden Retriever puppies act like? They like walks.

sit

They can learn to **sit**.

They like to run and play.

This puppy can fetch a ball.

Did you find these words?

They have long **ears**.

They have **golden** fur.

These are Golden Retriever **puppies**!

They can learn to **sit**.

Photo Glossary

 **ears** (eerz): The organs you hear with on either side of the head.

 **golden** (GOHL-duhn): A deep yellow color.

 **puppies** (PUHP-eez): Dogs that are young and not fully grown.

 **sit** (sit): To rest your weight on your hindquarters.

Index

fetch 13

fur 6

learn 11

play 12

run 12

walks 10

About the Author

Hailey Scragg is a writer from Ohio. She loves all puppies, especially her puppy, Abe! She likes taking him on long walks in the park.

www.rourkeeducationalmedia.com

PHOTO CREDITS: cover: ©Dixi_, ©manley099 (bone); back cover: ©Naddiya (pattern); back cover (inset), page 8: ©chayathonwong; pages 2, 3, 9, 14, 15: ©Bigandt_Photography; pages 2, 4-5, 14, 15: ©Paige_Rigoglioso; pages 2, 6-7, 14, 15: ©StudioByTheSea; page 10: ©skynesher; pages 2, 11, 14, 15: ©MarkoNOVKOV; pages 12-13: ©HollyAA

Edited by: Kim Thompson
Cover and interior design by: Janine Fisher

Library of Congress PCN Data
Golden Retriever Puppies / Hailey Scragg
(Top Puppies)
ISBN 978-1-73162-855-8 (hard cover)(alk. paper)
ISBN 978-1-73162-854-1 (soft cover)
ISBN 978-1-73162-857-2 (e-Book)
ISBN 978-1-73163-338-5 (ePub)
Library of Congress Control Number: 2019945499

Printed in the United States of America,
North Mankato, Minnesota